10
Money Habits That Will Keep You Poor Forever

Break Free From Poor Financial Management

By

Robert D. Gibson

Table Of Content

Introduction

Understanding The Impact Of Money Habits

Have you ever questioned why some people appear to amass a fortune with ease while others are constantly struggling to make ends meet? The answer often lies in their money habits. A habit is not merely an isolated action; it is a consistent behavioral pattern that shapes our daily routines and, ultimately, our outcomes. When it comes to money, our habits can determine whether we build a solid financial foundation or remain trapped in a cycle of financial insecurity.

These money habits are the small, seemingly insignificant choices we make daily that collectively determine our financial trajectory. They extend beyond simple budgeting and saving practices; they encompass our mindset, values, and approach to earnings, spending, and investing. Understanding and acknowledging these habits is the first step toward transforming your financial situation.

In this book, we will take an in-depth look at ten specific money habits that, if left unchecked, can keep you poor forever. Each chapter will address a different habit, offering insights into its negative impact and providing actionable steps to break free from its grip. From neglecting financial education to avoiding financial planning, we will explore the mindset and behaviors that perpetuate financial struggles and suggest alternative approaches to cultivate financial well-being.

It's important to remember that our relationship with money is deeply rooted in psychological, cultural, and societal factors. While changing these ingrained habits might not happen overnight, it is possible with commitment and guidance. Throughout this book, we will provide practical strategies, real-life examples, and exercises to help you shift your money habits and mindset toward a more prosperous future.

Whether you are someone who is currently experiencing financial difficulties, someone who wants to avoid falling into the traps of poor money management, or even someone who is already on a stable financial path but wants to enhance their wealth-building journey, this book is designed to offer valuable insights and actionable advice. By understanding the impact of these money habits, you can make intentional choices that align with your financial goals and aspirations.

In the following chapters, we will delve into each of the ten detrimental money habits, exploring their underlying causes, their effects on your financial well-being, and most importantly, how to replace them with constructive alternatives. Remember, achieving financial security and abundance is not about luck; it's about making conscious decisions and cultivating positive habits that lead to lasting prosperity. So, let's begin this journey of transformation and empowerment as we uncover the ten money habits that you can overcome to pave the way for a brighter financial future.

Habit 1: Neglecting Financial Education

It's amazing how often financial education takes a back place in our lives in a culture obsessed with money. The majority of us graduate from educational institutions with knowledge of history, science, and literature but with little knowledge of personal financial and money management. The absence of financial education is a major issue that can have far-reaching and long-term consequences for our financial well-being.

Financial Knowledge's Strength

In a world where money is so important, having financial knowledge is like having the key to a treasure mine of opportunity and security. While the subject of personal finance may appear intimidating or complex, the truth is that anyone willing to begin a journey of learning and understanding can harness the power of financial knowledge. The importance of financial education cannot be emphasized, from managing day-to-day spending to making informed investment decisions.

Understanding and Empowerment

Financial knowledge, at its heart, empowers individuals to take control of their financial destinies. Understanding the fundamentals of budgeting, saving, investing, and debt management lays the groundwork for making educated decisions that are consistent with one's goals and values. When you have financial knowledge, you have the tools to negotiate the often complex world of personal money.

Consider making a budget that not only covers your spending but also provides for savings and investments. Consider learning how to assess risks and potential returns on various investing options. This level of comprehension turns financial judgments from wild guesses to measured and well-informed ones. With financial knowledge, you can take command of your financial ship and drive it in the direction you want.

Getting Rid of Financial Stress

The lowering of financial concern is one of the most significant advantages of financial understanding. Many people are stressed and apprehensive about money, which is typically due to a lack of understanding. Financial language and sophisticated concepts can cause feelings of overwhelm, prompting many to avoid dealing with their finances entirely. This avoidance, on the other hand, exacerbates the situation.

When you devote time to learning about finances, you tear down the obstacles that contribute to anxiety. As you obtain clarity about your financial status and options, your dread of the unknown fades. With this newfound knowledge, you may devise plans to pay off debt, save for emergencies, and achieve financial objectives. This sense of purpose and control produces a sense of serenity and confidence that transcends beyond financial concerns.

Taking Advantage of Opportunities for Wealth Creation

Financial knowledge unlocks opportunities for wealth growth that would otherwise be hidden. For example, understanding the power of compound interest can change the trajectory of your savings and investments. Given enough time, a little investment can grow into a sizable sum. You may miss out on the opportunity to grow your wealth over time if you do not have this knowledge.

Furthermore, financial education enables you to objectively analyze various investment choices. Whether it's the stock market, real estate, or another investment vehicle, being able to assess risks and rewards allows you to make decisions that are consistent with your risk tolerance and financial objectives. This not only increases your chances of becoming wealthy, but it also protects you from falling victim to scams or improper investments.

Leaving a Financial Literacy Legacy
Financial knowledge is a never-ending gift. When you educate yourself on how money works and how to manage it efficiently, you

benefit not just yourself but future generations as well. You may help interrupt cycles of financial insecurity and set the groundwork for your family's financial success by practicing healthy financial habits and passing this knowledge along.

Early financial education instills a sense of responsibility and understanding in children and young adults. It provides them with abilities that will be extremely useful as they navigate their financial adventures. A family that emphasizes financial literacy creates an environment for open discussions about money, decreasing the stigma and secrecy that is frequently associated with finances.

Financial knowledge is a guiding light that illuminates the route to wealth in a world where financial decisions abound. The benefits of understanding personal finance are immeasurable, ranging from making educated decisions to lowering financial stress and capitalizing on possibilities for wealth growth. Regardless of where you are on your financial path, investing in your financial education is a step toward empowerment and security. Accept the opportunity to learn, grow, and transform your relationship with money, unlocking the door to a future of financial security and the ability to pursue your ambitions.

Consequences of Ignorance in Money Management

In a world where financial decisions have a huge impact on our lives, poor money management can have a wide range of negative implications. Failure to understand and efficiently manage your finances can lead to both short-term and long-term difficulties that impair your general well-being.

- **Debt accumulation:** The accumulation of debt is one of the most immediate and uncomfortable effects of financial ignorance. Individuals who are unfamiliar with budgeting, spending patterns, and interest rates may find themselves living over their means. Credit card debt, high-interest loans, and other forms of borrowing may quickly spiral out of control, trapping people in a cycle of debt that is difficult to break free from. Ignorance of how debt works and its possible effects can result in crippling financial stress and anxiety.

- **Limited Financial Opportunities:** Financial knowledge opens the door to a universe of possibilities that would otherwise be closed. You will miss out on the opportunity to generate wealth and safeguard your future if you do not grasp how to save, invest, and increase your money. Ignorance of investment options and techniques might result in missed opportunities for asset growth, leaving you with insufficient financial resources in times of need or retirement.

- **Inadequate Emergency Planning:** Financial crises, such as unexpected medical bills or job loss, can occur at any time. Money management ignorance frequently leads to a lack of emergency planning, leaving individuals susceptible when unexpected bills come. Without a safety net in place, these events can lead to even deeper financial difficulties, complicating an already difficult position.

- **Financial Goals Stability:** Setting and accomplishing financial goals can be difficult without a solid understanding of money management. Whether you're looking to buy a house, establish a business, or save for college, a lack of financial understanding can make it difficult to plan and execute your plans. Ignorance can lead to mistakes, missed chances, and a sense of helplessness when it comes to attaining your goals.

- **Relationships That Are Strained:** Financial stress is a major source of conflict in partnerships. Money management ignorance can lead to disputes, mistrust, and animosity among family members or partners. Conversations concerning financial difficulties are frequently avoided, resulting in secrecy and misconceptions that can undermine even the closest relationships.

- **Insecurity Regarding Retirement:** A lack of financial awareness can have disastrous consequences for your retirement. Ignorance regarding retirement planning, pension alternatives, and investing techniques might lead to insufficient savings. Individuals are thus ill-prepared to maintain their desired lifestyle in their elder years, potentially requiring them to work longer or live with financial restraints during their retirement.

- **Missed Wealth-Building Opportunities:** The power of compound interest and judicious investments can have a substantial impact on your wealth over time. Ignorance in money management leads to missed opportunities to capitalize on the potential of these financial tools. Without adequate understanding, you may settle for low-yielding savings accounts and miss out on opportunities that may triple your financial resources.

Poor money management can have far-reaching implications that affect many facets of your life. The consequences of not understanding how to handle your finances can be serious, ranging from increasing debt and missed financial opportunities to strained relationships and insufficient retirement preparation. To prevent negative effects and promote financial well-being, it is critical to devote time and effort to developing a basic understanding of personal finance fundamentals. By doing so, you empower yourself to make informed decisions, establish a solid financial foundation, and create a brighter future for yourself and your loved ones.

Habit 2: Relying on a Single Income Source

In a world of unpredictability and rapid change, relying entirely on one source of income can be a risky and restricting financial approach. While having solid employment or a major source of income is vital for fulfilling your immediate requirements, putting all of your financial eggs in one basket might leave you vulnerable to a variety of obstacles and failures. Diversifying your revenue streams is not only a wise financial move; it is also an important step toward creating resilience and protecting your financial future.

Diversification and Financial Security

In the world of banking, the phrase "don't put all your eggs in one basket" could not be more true. Diversification, also known as the golden rule of investing, is a practical and strong technique that can considerably improve your financial stability. It is not a complicated financial term reserved for professionals; rather, it is a practical principle that anyone can apply to their investing strategy.

Diversification, at its foundation, involves spreading your investments over a variety of assets to lessen risk. The concept is simple: when one investment underperforms or has a downturn, the impact on your whole portfolio is mitigated because other assets are likely to perform differently. You construct a safety net for your investments by combining assets that react differently to market conditions.

Managing Risk: Investing involves risk. Diversification, on the other hand, helps you manage and limit that risk. Instead of placing all of your money into a single investment that may change substantially, you spread your money across several categories. For example, you may have a mix of equities, bonds, real estate, and possibly even alternative investments like commodities. This diversification aids in the overall success of your portfolio.

Balancing Your Portfolio: Diversification does not include picking investments at random. It is about developing a balanced combination that corresponds to your financial objectives, risk tolerance, and investment horizon. Different investments have varying levels of risk and possible return. To strike the correct balance between stability and possible growth, a diversified portfolio could comprise both conservative, income-generating assets and growth-oriented higher-risk investments.

Avoiding Overconcentration: Putting all of your money into one or a few assets can be tempting, especially if they've produced spectacular returns in the past. This method, though, can put you in danger. Consider the possibility that a single company's stock would drop, causing your entire investment to plummet. Diversification helps you prevent overconcentration in a single investment, saving you from catastrophic losses.

Managing Market Volatility: Financial markets are notorious for their volatility. Economic causes, geopolitical events, and unexpected news can all cause market volatility. Diversification acts as a protection against such volatility. While one asset may be harmed by a specific incident, others in your portfolio may remain stable or even prosper, mitigating the overall impact on your assets.

Creating a Long-Term Strategy: Diversification is not a one-time activity; it is a continuing approach. Your portfolio will need to be adjusted as your objectives and market conditions change. Regularly monitoring and rebalancing your investments ensures that your diversification plan stays effective and in line with your goals.

Begin Small And Steady: Diversification might be intimidating to new investors. You don't have to dive in headfirst. Begin small and steady. Begin by purchasing a diversified mutual fund or exchange-traded fund (ETF). These funds pool money from several investors to invest in a variety of assets, offering you rapid exposure to diversification without the burden of managing multiple investments.

Seek Professional Advice: While diversity is a realistic strategy, it can be difficult to apply effectively. Seeking advice from a financial advisor or investing specialist might be advantageous. They may assist you in assessing your financial goals, risk tolerance, and investment timeframe to develop a diversified portfolio tailored to your specific scenario.

Diversification is a practical strategy that allows you to traverse the volatile waters of finance with greater confidence and security. It's not about anticipating market swings; it's about preparing for them. By diversifying your investments, you're laying a solid financial foundation that can withstand storms and capture chances. Whether you're a new or seasoned investor, embracing diversity as a practical method will put you on the path to better financial security and success.

Exploring Multiple Income Streams in Realistic Ways

The idea of relying entirely on one source of income is gradually fading from relevance in today's unpredictable and dynamic economic environment. It has become clear that exploring several sources of income is a realistic and strategic way to increase financial security, accomplish your goals, and seize new chances. Here are some doable strategies to diversify your income streams, whether you're wanting to increase your present income or start down the path to financial independence.

1. Freelancing And Side Businesses: Getting a side job or starting to freelance is one of the easiest ways to start making extra money. You can market your abilities and services to a global clientele through websites like Upwork, Fiverr, and TaskRabbit. A market exists for your skills whether you're a writer, graphic designer, programmer, or handyman. Your side business can potentially develop into a sizeable source of revenue by starting small and steadily growing your clientele.

2. Investments In Real Estate: Real estate investing is a tried-and-true way to make passive income. Real estate can offer a reliable source of income in the form of rental payments or dividends, whether it's used to rent out a home, lease commercial space, or invest in real estate crowdfunding platforms. Even though it necessitates an initial outlay, it can prove to be a successful long-term tactic.

3. Investments and Stocks Paying Dividends: Without having to sell your assets, investing in dividend-paying stocks and income-focused investment vehicles can give you consistent distributions. Established corporations with dividend stocks frequently split a percentage of their profits with shareholders, generating a steady flow of income. In a similar vein, over time, bonds and specific investment vehicles can also produce reliable income.

4. Online Companies And Online Shopping: Online company endeavors now have a vast array of prospects thanks to the growth of e-commerce. The internet offers a global market for your goods whether you're dropshipping, selling homemade crafts, or opening an e-commerce store. Setting up an internet business and reaching a large consumer base is now simpler than ever thanks to platforms like Shopify, Etsy, and Amazon.

5. Asset Rental Income: You can get rental income from assets and other real estate as well. This may entail renting out tools, automobiles, or even your own space for gatherings or events. With the help of websites like Airbnb, you can earn money from your underutilized space by renting out a spare room or your entire house to tourists.

6. Online Courses and Products: Consider producing and selling digital items like e-books, online courses, or tutorials if you are an expert in a particular industry. You may make a passive income while sharing your knowledge and abilities with a global audience through websites like Udemy and Teachable.

7. Crowdfunding And Peer-To-Peer Lending: Crowdfunding and peer-to-peer financing websites give users the chance to participate in loans or projects in return for interest payments or a cut of profits. This can offer a largely hands-off approach to making money while supporting projects that are in line with your interests.

8. Affiliate Promotion: Affiliate marketing can be a successful way to earn commissions by promoting goods or services from other businesses if you have a blog, website, or social media following. A portion of sales made via your exclusive affiliate links belong to you.

9. Lease Your Property: Consider renting out any valuable things you own if you don't utilize them all the time. You might be able to do this by renting out your camera gear, power tools, or even your car. Local communities and peer-to-peer networks can enable you to connect with people in need of short-term access to your assets.

10. Launch A Podcast Or A Youtube Channel: The development of content provides a variety of economic prospects in the digital age. Starting a podcast or YouTube channel and building a following can allow you to earn money through sponsorships, merchandise sales, crowdfunding from your devoted fans, and advertising.

12. Platforms For The Gig Economy: Multiple flexible earning alternatives have been made available by the gig economy. These systems, which range from meal delivery services like DoorDash and Uber Eats to ride-sharing services like Uber and Lyft, let you work when you choose.

The path to financial freedom and security is best traveled with a multifaceted strategy. Finding additional sources of income not only improves your financial stability but also creates new opportunities for development and fulfillment on a personal level. By varying your sources of income, you can better withstand economic changes and seize the opportunity for a better financial future in addition to growing your income.

Habit 3: Living Beyond Your Means

It's simple to live beyond your means in a culture that frequently elevates materialism and consumption. Even though it can be alluring to buy the newest technology, and fashionable clothing, and eat at hip restaurants, the effects of continually spending more than you make can be harmful to your financial stability.

The Risk of Spending Too Much: How to Avoid Financial Instability

The danger of overspending lies menacingly beneath the surface of our financial lives in a world that relentlessly bombards us with commercials, promotions, and a culture of consumerism. Spending consistently more than your income is known as overspending. While it may appear harmless at first, the effects of overspending can affect every element of your financial well-being. Let's explore the risks of excessive spending and the negative effects it can have on your long-term goals, mental health, and financial security.

Understanding the Temptation

The temptation of excessive spending frequently results from a variety of internal and environmental reasons. Modern marketing strategies are intended to arouse cravings, encouraging the notion that owning the newest technology, and fashionable clothing, and dining at hip restaurants are necessary for a fulfilling life. In addition, cultural pressures and the need to preserve one's image in the era of social media may lead people to engage in a cycle of spending that is much outside of their means.

Internally, the sensation of satisfaction and achievement that comes with buying something new can be contagious. This emotional response may become compulsive, resulting in repetitive actions that eventually develop into a pattern of excessive spending.

1. A Harmful Debt Cycle

Overspending frequently starts a debt cycle that can be challenging to escape. These behaviors, such as using credit cards to the limit, taking out loans for non-essential expenditures, or relying extensively on buy-now-pay-later plans, can result in a growing debt load. The issue is exacerbated by high-interest rates on credit card debt and loans, making it difficult to get out of the hole financially.

At first, the rush of immediate enjoyment could obscure the truth of the looming financial load. But as time goes on, the burden of debt gets heavier and heavier. Your income is steadily depleted by rising monthly expenses, which limit your financial flexibility. Debt buildup can deteriorate your general well-being by causing you to feel helpless, anxious, and even ashamed.

2. Financial Anxiety and Stress

The increased amount of financial stress and anxiety that overspending generates is one of the most noticeable effects. Your mental health may suffer as a result of persistent stress about bills, making minimum payments, or figuring out how to pay for things. Your relationships, professional performance, and a general sense of well-being can all be impacted by this stress, which can penetrate every part of your existence.

A vicious cycle might result from financial stress. Ineffective coping strategies, like overspending, may be triggered by stress itself, which in turn makes it worse. When this cycle takes control, you could feel stuck and overtaken by your financial condition.

3. Negating Financial Objectives

Spending excessively can undermine your efforts to reach your financial objectives. Whether you're trying to save for a house, prepare for retirement, or pay off student loans, every dollar wasted is money that could have gone toward your objectives. Small, pointless purchases made over time can take money away from your goals in a significant way.

Take the desire to acquire a home, for instance. You need to be consistent and disciplined when saving for a down payment.

Overspending, however, might deplete your savings, postponing your goal of becoming a homeowner. It can get harder and harder to put off current demands in favor of future necessities, which might frustrate you and cause your financial progress to stagnate.

4. Long-Term Satisfaction vs. Temporary Pleasure

Spending too much is frequently the result of prioritizing instant delight above long-term satisfaction. A momentary feeling of enjoyment can be obtained through an impulsive shopping trip or a pricey restaurant meal. However, this enjoyment is frequently fleeting, and the long-term financial repercussions may cause regret and greater unhappiness.

It's simple to overlook the greater picture in the quest for worldly goods. The accumulation of material items that deteriorate in value over time may overshadow the experiences and memories that bring fulfillment. Instead of the acquisition of material possessions, long-lasting enjoyment frequently results from experiences, personal development, and meaningful connections.

5. Relationship Stress

Relationship stress is frequently a result of financial disputes. Without clear communication and agreed-upon financial goals, overspending can strain relationships and cause arguments and resentment. The foundation of trust and cohesion can be undermined by misaligned spending patterns and financial priorities since they might cause a rift between partners.

Arguments, mistrust, and feelings of betrayal can result from a lack of financial transparency. In other circumstances, one partner may be solely responsible for excessive spending, which can harm their financial situation and the relationship. In extreme circumstances, this can result in a breakdown in communication, emotional isolation, and even separation.

6. Financially Constrained

Living above your means keeps you trapped in a cycle of constant spending to keep up appearances and pay off debts. You are unable to make decisions that are consistent with your ideals and aspirations because of your lack of financial independence. True financial independence entails the capacity to seize chances, take measured risks, and live your life as you choose.

The capacity to make decisions that are not mainly influenced by financial considerations is a component of financial independence. Financial freedom enables you to live life according to your ideals rather than being restricted by financial commitments, whether that be engaging in a passion, traveling the world, or investing in personal growth.

Making a Sustainable Budget

aking a sustainable budget is a crucial first step in achieving financial stability and empowerment in a world where financial landscapes are always changing. A budget is more than simply a list of numbers; it's a roadmap that directs your spending, enables you to match your priorities with your expenditure, and paves the way for long-term success. Let's talk about why making a sustainable budget is important and how to put it at the center of your financial path.

Understanding a Budget's Core Concepts

A budget is a thorough plan that details your expected income and expenses for a certain period, usually monthly. It gives you a comprehensive picture of your financial condition, empowering you to allocate funds sensibly, keep an eye on your spending habits, and work toward your financial objectives. A well-designed budget serves as a road map for your finances, guiding you as you negotiate the complexity of regular costs, savings, and investments.

A Sustainable Budget Has These Advantages

Financial Sense You may see your cash inflows and outflows with the help of a budget. You can find areas where you can reduce or optimize your expenditure since it takes the guessing out of where your money is going and gives you clarity on where it is going.

- Goal Achievement: Having a budget in place will allow you to devote money toward your objectives, whether they are debt repayment, vacation savings, or retirement investing. Making conscious resource allocations and working toward your goals are made possible by creating a budget.

- Debt management: Maintaining a workable budget enables you to make timely payments on your debts. You may consistently move closer to debt freedom by setting aside a portion of your salary for debt repayment.

- Emergency Planning: Having a budget with provisions for an emergency fund gives you a safety net to handle unforeseen financial difficulties without jeopardizing your long-term financial ambitions.

- Reduced Stress: Uncertainty and a lack of control are common causes of financial stress. A budget gives you financial control, reducing the stress and worry that comes with financial concerns.

- Planning for the Future: A budget promotes long-term thinking. It encourages you to save away money for upcoming necessities like retirement, education, and large purchases to make sure you're ready for what's to come.

Making a Sustainable Budget: Steps to Take

- Determine Your Income: Calculate your monthly income total, taking into account your pay, earnings from side jobs, and any other income you may have.

- Describe the fixed costs: Determine your fixed expenses, which remain the same every month. Utility bills, rent or mortgage payments, insurance fees, and loan payments are a few examples.

- Keep track of variable costs: Keep track of your variable costs, which could change each month. These can include spending on food, entertainment, dining out, and other luxuries.

- Invest in Savings: Set aside a portion of your salary for savings and investing to make saving a priority. This could entail making payments into retirement accounts, emergency savings accounts, and other financial objectives.

- Plan for Debt Repayment: If you have any unpaid debts, set aside money in your budget to pay them off. To reduce interest payments, concentrate on paying off high-interest debt first.

- Make spending categories to better understand where your money is going by classifying your expenses. It is simpler to find places where you can make savings thanks to this categorization.

- Set Realistic Limits: When establishing your budget, be honest with yourself about the amount you can spend. Overly ambitious goals increase the risk of budget abandonment and might cause frustration.

- Watch and Modify: Review your budget frequently to make sure you're on course. Make the required modifications if you find differences between your anticipated and actual spending.

- Include Every Member of the Family: Include family members or housemates in the budgeting process if you split spending with them. By working together, everyone's wants and priorities are taken into account.
- Accept Flexibility: Unexpected changes are a part of life. Allow your budget to be adaptable enough to account for unforeseen circumstances while yet adhering to your financial objectives.

Developing Long-Term Financial Routines

Making a sustainable budget requires a continuing commitment to careful financial management; it is not a one-time exercise. Keep these guidelines in mind as you set out on this journey:

- Start Modestly: If you've never created a budget before, start with one that only includes your important costs. Expanding and fine-tuning your budget as you gain comfort is a good idea.

- Have Patience: Getting used to a budget may take some time and work. Be kind to yourself as you develop the ability to efficiently balance your income and expenses.

- Recognize Progress: Every action you take to improve your money management is a success. Celebrate your accomplishments, whether they involve paying off debt or accumulating a certain amount of savings.

- Understand and Adapt: Your budget might need to be modified if your financial condition changes. Be willing to learn about your shifting requirements and goals so that you may adjust your budget accordingly.

- Put Values First: Align your spending plan with your priorities and core values. This makes sure that your spending matches what is important to you, increasing your sense of fulfillment in life as a whole.

The dynamic process of developing a sustainable budget gives you the power to take charge of your financial future. You can improve your financial stability, reduce stress, and realize your most valued goals by comprehending the fundamentals of budgeting, appreciating its advantages, and adopting a proactive approach to financial management. Keep in mind that a budget is a tool that allows you to make deliberate decisions and create your financial destiny, not a limitation.

Habit 4: Not Tracking Your Expenses

It's simple to allow your spending habits to become automatic in the rush of modern life, especially if you aren't actively keeping track of your spending. However, failing to keep track of where your money is going can have a significant impact on both your overall well-being and financial situation. Let's explore the dangers of not keeping track of your spending and discover why maintaining sound financial judgment is an essential component of good money management.

The Importance of Expense Tracking

Keeping track of your expenses gives you insights into your spending patterns, gives you the power to make wise decisions, and directs you toward attaining your financial objectives. Tracking your spending is an essential step on the road to financial success, whether your goals are better budgeting, debt elimination, or saving for significant milestones. Let's talk about the importance of cost reporting and how it might improve your financial perspective.

1. Awareness and Transparency

Tracking your expenses makes your financial situation very clear. It sheds light on your spending habits, highlighting patterns and trends that you might have missed otherwise. You can acquire a complete insight into your spending patterns, from necessary expenses to luxuries, by classifying your expenses.

You can spot places where you're overspending thanks to your increased awareness, which gives you the chance to consciously make changes. It's a reality check that destroys the delusion of financial security and replaces it with precise financial health insights.

2. Knowledge for Empowerment

In the world of personal finance, the proverb "knowledge is power" remains true. By keeping track of your spending, you give yourself the information you need to make wise decisions. When you have information about your spending patterns, you may improve your financial plan, proactively handle any financial imbalances, and allocate resources following your priorities.

You can foresee future expenses and prepare for them by using expense tracking. Knowing about these upcoming financial commitments can help you prevent financial stress at the last minute, whether it is for a significant purchase, a trip, or the renewal of an annual membership.

3. Accuracy in Budgeting

Financial security is built on having a budget, and keeping track of expenses accurately is a crucial part of budgeting. When you keep track of your expenses, you are using facts rather than just an estimate of your spending. With more accuracy, your budget is more effective since you may allocate money according to your actual financial actions.

Your spending will be in line with your financial objectives if your budget is well-made. By ensuring that your budget truly represents your lifestyle, expense monitoring makes it simpler to manage your money wisely and prevent overspending.

4. Effective Debt Reduction

Keeping track of expenses is a smart move for anyone trying to reduce their debt. You can find places where you can make savings and put more money toward paying off debt by keeping an eye on your spending. Your efforts to pay off debt might be significantly impacted by the money you save by cutting back on discretionary expenses.

Additionally, keeping track of your spending helps you stick to your debt payback strategy. It keeps you on track toward your financial objectives by preventing you from deviating due to irrational expenditure.

5. Maximizing Savings

Not only does expense tracking highlight extravagance, but it also identifies areas where money can be saved. When you keep track of little, recurrent expenses, you can find places to make savings without compromising your quality of life. little, recurring expenses can mount up without your awareness.

Savings go beyond just cutting costs; they also include making the most of your investments. You can designate money for different savings goals, such as retirement, emergency reserves, and future dreams after you have a clear grasp of your discretionary income.

6. A Financial Skill for Life

Keeping track of your expenses is a lifelong skill rather than a one-time task. Your spending monitoring procedures will vary to reflect changes in your income, goals, and priorities as your financial situation changes. You can navigate financial difficulties, grasp opportunities, and develop a stable financial future by being able to track and control your expenses.

Instruments and Techniques for Successful Expense Monitoring

Financial management requires careful spending monitoring since it gives you the information you need to make wise choices and reach your financial objectives. Fortunately, there are several tools and techniques available to make tracking your costs easier and more efficient. You can use these tools to better understand your spending habits, spot areas for development, and take charge of your financial security.

- **Financial Apps:** The way people track their money has been completely transformed by budgeting apps. You may enter your income and organize your expenses using these apps' user-friendly interfaces. They frequently link with your credit cards and bank accounts, classifying transactions automatically and displaying graphic representations of your spending patterns. You Need A Budget, PocketGuard, and Mint are a few well-known budgeting applications.

- **Spreadsheets:** Spreadsheets are a useful tool for spending tracking if you'd rather take a more active approach. You can develop a personalized spending tracking spreadsheet using applications like Microsoft Excel or Google Sheets. Organize the date, description, category, and expenditure amount into columns. With the manual method, you may customize the spreadsheet to meet your unique demands and have creative control over its design.

- **Embedded System:** The envelope system is a cash-based approach to managing expenses that entails designating actual envelopes for various spending categories. You put a specific amount of money in each envelope at the start of the month. You stop making purchases in that category for the month once the money in an envelope has been used. This approach offers a practical means of controlling discretionary expenditure and averting excess.

- **Statements For Credit Cards:** For cardholders, credit card statements act as a built-in spending tracking tool. These statements list each credit card transaction and group it into several spending categories. Reviewing your credit card statement can nevertheless give you insights into your spending patterns and habits even though it is less proactive than other approaches. To use this strategy, each transaction must be carefully examined and classified.

- **Tracking Manually And Receipts:** Tracking spending manually can be done simply yet effectively by gathering and sorting receipts. Keep every receipt you receive, and routinely classify them according to the spending categories you've chosen. This approach demands restraint and reliability but provides a concrete record of your expenditures.

- **Online Alerts and Banking:** The tools that categorize your transactions and provide spending summaries are available on many online banking platforms. Some banks also let you set up notifications for particular expenditure thresholds, which might help you keep within your spending limit.

- **Photo-taking Apps:** You can take pictures of your receipts and keep them digitally using photography apps. This approach gives you a well-organized record of your costs while doing away with the need to physically collect receipts. You may simply categorize receipts by taking images of them using apps like Expensify and Evernote.

- **Regular Reflection And Review:** Regardless of the methods you select, constant assessment and reflection are essential to efficient spending management. Set aside time each week or month to check over your recorded costs, look for patterns, and gauge how well you're doing in terms of your financial objectives. You may distribute resources, change your budget, and make informed judgments as a result of this reflection.

Effective spending monitoring can be accomplished using a variety of tools and techniques that suit different interests and lifestyles. The objective is the same, whether you choose more manual methods like spreadsheets and envelopes or technology-driven ones like budgeting apps: you want to obtain a clear picture of your financial practices and align your spending with your goals. By using these tools, you give yourself the power to take charge of your money, make deliberate decisions, and start along the path to financial success.

Habit 5: Having a Poverty Mindset

A scarcity mentality, often referred to as a poverty mindset, is a way of thinking that is characterized by the conviction that there will never be enough of anything, be it money, opportunity, or resources. People who have a poverty mindset frequently believe that there are limits to the universe and that they are helpless to alter their situation. This self-limiting thinking system may have a significant impact on a person's possibilities, financial choices, and general well-being. Unlocking an abundance attitude and embracing a future full of opportunities require recognizing and overcoming a poverty perspective.

Recognizing Negative Financial Beliefs

Our beliefs influence our reality, and this is particularly true when it comes to money. Negative financial ideas can operate as imperceptible roadblocks that restrict our potential, sway our judgment, and obstruct our path to financial success. These engrained opinions are frequently the result of early encounters, societal influences, and cultural indoctrination. Financial empowerment, overcoming self-imposed constraints, and building a more promising financial future all depend on recognizing and dealing with these unfavorable ideas.

The Influence of Belief

Our worldview is filtered through our beliefs. They shape the outcomes we encounter by influencing our ideas, feelings, and behaviors. Conscious or unconscious, unfavorable financial assumptions can have a big impact on our actions and outcomes. They turn into self-fulfilling prophecies, supporting our prejudices and influencing how we view chances and difficulties.

Commonly Held Financial Myths

- The saying "Money is the Root of Evil" is frequently based on misunderstandings of a well-known biblical passage. A belief that money is intrinsically bad can cause guilt about financial achievement and avoidance of opportunities to develop wealth.
- The self-limiting idea that "I'm not good with money" prevents people from managing their money wisely or seeking out financial education.
- "Money Is Limited": Having a scarcity mindset, which makes people feel motivated to hoard money rather than invest it or share it, might result from

thinking that there is only a limited quantity of money accessible.

- "I'll Never Be Wealthy": This conviction frequently results from comparing oneself to others or from previous financial difficulties. It may deter people from pursuing wealth-accumulation plans and taking reasonable risks.

- "Financial Success Requires Sacrificing Happiness" When people think that achieving financial success means sacrificing their happiness, they may unconsciously sabotage their efforts to advance their finances.

- "It's Too Late to Start": People who hold this idea are discouraged from taking action to better their financial status because they believe that if they didn't start early, they will miss the chance to succeed financially.

Identifying False Beliefs

- Self-Reflection: Spend some time reflecting on your beliefs and emotions toward money. Are there any persistent negative feelings or thoughts? Finding these patterns can reveal hidden limiting beliefs.

- Personality Types: Keep an eye on your spending habits. Do you routinely put off doing financial duties like investing or creating a budget? These behaviors can expose underlying false ideas.

- An emotional response: Pay close attention to how you feel when you talk about money. You may have underlying unfavorable ideas that are causing your fear, guilt, or avoidance.

- Triggers: Some discussions or circumstances can make people believe bad things about money. Recognize these triggers, then consider why they cause the reactions they do.

- Previous Experiences Consider your previous financial experiences and how they may have shaped your attitudes. Were there any events that influenced the way you think now?

Taking Care of Negative Beliefs

- Dispute the Belief: Examine the veracity of your unfavorable beliefs. Are they founded on genuine data or just conjecture? Put these assumptions to the test with logical, convincing counterarguments.

- Reframe: Change your negative thoughts into positive statements. As an example, you may alter "I'm not good with money" to "I am able to learn and improve my financial skills."

- Obtain Education: Learn as much as you can about personal finance. Knowing more equips you to disprove false beliefs with evidence and workable solutions.

- Practice mindfulness to become aware of unfavorable ideas as they enter your head. Once they are recognized, intentionally decide to replace them with constructive options.

- Visualization: Envision yourself succeeding financially and dispelling the limiting ideas that have prevented you.

- Professional Assistance: If unfavorable views are pervasive in your life and affecting your everyday activities, think about getting professional assistance, such as therapy or counseling.

Creating Financial Beliefs That Are Empowering

- Select Beneficial Role Models: Be in the company of people who have sound financial attitudes and practices.

- Recognize and enjoy your financial successes, no matter how modest they may be. This strengthens your confidence and supports your good beliefs.

- Practice affirmations to gradually reprogram your subconscious thought. Repeat positive statements about money regularly.

- Set Realistic Objectives: Setting and attaining financial objectives helps you replace negative self-talk with positive self-affirmation by providing concrete proof of your talents.

- Continuous Learning: Keep an open mind and strive to increase your financial literacy. Building strong educational foundations is essential for developing optimistic financial beliefs.

Financial empowerment and progress can only occur when negative financial beliefs are acknowledged and addressed. You may transform your financial reality and embrace a future full of opportunity by discovering these hidden restrictions, questioning their veracity, and replacing them with empowering ideas.

Developing a Wealth-Oriented Mindset

A wealth-oriented mindset is a potent stimulant for financial success and opens up a world of possibilities. A wealth-oriented mindset welcomes plenty, possibilities, and the conviction that you can generate and attract riches, as opposed to a scarcity or poverty mindset, which focuses on restrictions and lack. You may transform your financial journey, make educated decisions, and pave the route for a more affluent future by adopting this mentality.

1. Change Your Wealth Perspective: Begin by rethinking your concept of riches. While financial abundance is important, wealth also includes things like health, relationships, personal growth, and experiences. Accept a holistic definition of wealth that corresponds to your values and embraces all aspects of your life.

2. Embrace Abundance Thinking: Abundance thinking is the foundation of a wealth-oriented worldview. Instead of focusing on scarcity and restrictions, choose to perceive opportunities, possibilities, and growth potential. Believe that there is an abundance in the cosmos and that there is plenty for everyone.

3. Establish Specific Financial Objectives: Define your financial objectives clearly and precisely. Having well-defined goals provides direction and purpose, whether it's saving for a dream vacation, purchasing a home, or reaching financial independence. Create a plan to achieve these goals by breaking them down into concrete stages.

4. Create a Positive Money Relationship: Change your relationship with money from one of stress or fear to one of positivity and empowerment. Consider money to be a tool that can assist you in creating the life you want, supporting your beliefs, and providing possibilities for growth.

5. Constantly Educate Yourself: On the route to prosperity, knowledge is a potent instrument. Spend time learning about personal finance, investing, and wealth-building tactics. Continuous learning allows you to make more informed judgments and capitalize on possibilities.

6. Surround Yourself With Positive People: Surround yourself with others who share your wealth-focused mindset. Connect with people who will inspire and encourage you in your financial endeavors. Avoid negativity and critics who could sabotage your efforts.

7. Exercise Gratitude: Gratitude attracts abundance. Express thanks for the resources, opportunities, and experiences you have regularly. Gratitude changes your attention away from what is lacking and onto what is currently there in your life.

8. Visualize Your Achievement: Many successful people use visualization as a powerful approach. Spend some time each day visualizing yourself accomplishing your financial objectives. Consider the sentiments of accomplishment, security, and liberation that accompany financial success.

9. Embrace Healthy Risk-Taking: Wealthy people who are willing to take calculated risks. Recognize that progress and growth frequently necessitate venturing outside of your comfort zone. Educate yourself about potential risks and rewards, and then make informed decisions that are in line with your objectives.

10. Exercise Resilience: Challenges and setbacks are unavoidable on any road, including the path to wealth. Develop resilience by viewing mistakes as opportunities to learn. Instead of giving up, use setbacks to fine-tune your strategies and persevere.

11. Take Bold Action: A wealth-oriented attitude entails more than just positive thinking; it also entails taking regular, inspired action. Make plans, set your intentions, and then take serious measures toward your goals. Momentum is created by doing action.

12. Avoid Making Comparisons: When you compare yourself to others, you may experience thoughts of inadequacy or envy. Instead of comparing yourself to others, concentrate on your progress and growth.

13. Exercise Generosity: Giving back and being generous can help to strengthen your wealth-oriented mindset. Accept the idea that as you give, you will also receive. Generosity generates pleasant energy, whether through charity giving, volunteering, or supporting others.

14. Learn from Mistakes: Failures serve as springboards to success. Accept failures as great learning opportunities that contribute to your development and wisdom. Adjust your strategies in light of what you've learned, and press on with fresh zeal.

15. Rejoice in Your Victories: Celebrate your accomplishments, no matter how minor. Recognize your accomplishments and be proud of the steps you've taken toward financial plenty. Celebrating victories increases your confidence in your potential to achieve more.

Developing a wealth-oriented attitude is a journey that takes deliberate effort and perseverance. You can improve your relationship with money and create a financially prosperous future by changing your viewpoint, embracing abundance, making clear goals, and taking active steps. Remember that your mindset determines your reality, and adopting a wealth-oriented mindset opens the door to limitless possibilities and lays the groundwork for long-term success.

Habit 6: Failure To Invest

Not investing is a financial decision with long-term ramifications for your financial well-being. While it may appear to be more convenient to put your money in a savings account or to avoid the intricacies of investing, the reality is that failing to invest can result in missed opportunities, limited wealth building, and an inability to keep up with inflation. Let's look at why not investing can stifle your financial growth and what you might be missing out on by not taking advantage of investment opportunities.

Why is Investing Important for Wealth Creation?

Investing is more than just a financial plan; it is a crucial foundation for creating long-term wealth and financial freedom. While it is necessary to save money, focusing only on savings can limit your financial growth over time. Investing, on the other hand, puts your money to work for you, allowing for exponential development and long-term financial security. Let's look at why investing is important for wealth creation and why you should embrace this important financial habit.

1. Using Compound Interest to Your Advantage

Compound interest is often referred to as the "eighth wonder of the world" due to its extraordinary potential to build significant wealth over time. When you invest, your original contributions generate returns, which generate additional returns. This compounding impact snowballs your wealth, resulting in exponential growth that regular savings alone cannot achieve. Compound interest has a stronger influence on your financial portfolio the longer your money is invested.

2. Overcoming Inflation

Inflation, or the gradual increase in the cost of goods and services, reduces the purchasing power of your money. Saving money in a low-interest savings account may appear secure, but it cannot keep up with inflation. Investing allows you to potentially outrun inflation, keeping the true value of your money and ensuring its purchasing power over time.

3. Risk Management Diversification

Investing helps you to diversify your portfolio by allocating assets to several asset classes such as stocks, bonds, real estate, and commodities. Diversification mitigates the impact of a single investment's bad performance. When you spread risk across several assets, you reduce your exposure to market volatility. A well-diversified investing strategy protects your wealth and ensures stability during economic downturns.

4. Activation of Multiple Income Streams

Investing can generate additional income streams in addition to your core wages. These income sources add to your financial stability and ability to fulfill your financial goals, whether through dividends, rental income from real estate, or interest payments from bonds. Multiple streams of income not only boost your overall cash flow but also act as a safety net in the event of unforeseen financial difficulties.

5. Achieving Long-Term Financial Objectives

Investing can help you reach your long-term financial objectives, from retirement planning to important life events like buying a home or supporting college. A systematic approach to investing allows you to progressively accumulate the necessary finances. Whether you're planning for your own or your children's future, investments can help you make your dreams a reality.

6. Increasing Retirement Security

Individuals are more responsible for retirement preparation as traditional pension schemes become less frequent. Investing in retirement plans such as 401(k)s and IRAs provide tax benefits as well as the opportunity for big growth. These investments ensure that you have a happy and secure retirement, allowing you to spend your senior years worry-free.

7. Dealing with Economic Ups and Downs

The economy goes through cycles of expansion and decline. Investing assists you in navigating these cycles by setting your portfolio to profit from both upswings and downturns. While market volatility can be frightening, a well-planned investing strategy takes these changes into account and seeks to maximize long-term profits.

Investing isn't only for the wealthy; it's a must-do for anyone trying to grow money, protect their future, and achieve financial freedom. Investing, through the power of compound interest, diversification, and strategic planning, has the potential for enormous returns that savings alone cannot reach. Taking a proactive approach to investing puts you on track to create long-term wealth, achieve your financial goals, and experience a brighter and more affluent future.

Various Investment Options to Suit Different Risk Appetites

Investing is a unique path that is determined by your financial objectives, time horizon, and risk tolerance. Because everyone's risk tolerance varies, it's critical to select investing options that match your risk tolerance. Here are some investment possibilities classified by risk tolerance:

Investing with Low Risk:

- Savings Accounts: These are the most risk-free investment options. Savings accounts offer a guaranteed return, albeit one that is often smaller than that of other investing options. They're good for short-term goals and keeping an emergency fund.

- CDs: CDs offer somewhat greater interest rates than savings accounts, but your money is tied in for a certain length of time. They are considered low-risk, particularly if you choose FDIC-insured CDs.
- Treasury Bonds: Treasury bonds are issued by the United States government and are backed by the government's full faith and credit. They provide fixed-interest payments and are regarded as safe investments.

Moderate Risk Investments

- Bonds: Corporate bonds and municipal bonds provide larger yields than low-risk options but carry a somewhat higher risk. Companies offer corporate bonds, whereas state and local governments issue municipal bonds.
- Index Funds: These are mutual funds that seek to mirror the performance of a

certain market index. They provide diversification and are less risky than individual equities.

- Dividend Stocks: Dividend stocks provide income through monthly dividend payments. While there is some risk associated with them owing to market swings, they can provide a consistent revenue stream.

High-Risk Investment

- Stocks are a high-risk investment since they have the potential for high profits but also have a high level of volatility. Stock prices can fluctuate significantly, making them appropriate for individuals with higher risk tolerance.

- Real Estate Investment Trusts (REITs): REITs allow you to invest in real estate without actually owning it. They have the potential for capital appreciation as well as dividend income, but they are susceptible to real estate market movements.

- Commodities: While investing in commodities such as gold, silver, or oil might give diversification benefits, their prices are subject to global supply and demand dynamics.
- Cryptocurrencies, such as Bitcoin and Ethereum, have grown in popularity as high-risk, high-reward investments. They are notorious for their extraordinary volatility and should only be considered by individuals with an extremely high-risk tolerance.

Managed and Balanced Funds:
- Target-Date Funds: These are mutual funds that are designed to help with retirement planning. They alter their asset allocation automatically based on your planned retirement year,

becoming more conservative as you approach retirement.

- Balanced funds invest in a combination of equities and bonds, providing a balanced approach to risk and potential rewards.

Investment possibilities vary greatly to accommodate different risk tolerances. Your investment decisions should be based on your financial goals, time horizon, and level of comfort with probable value swings. To properly manage risk, it is critical to diversify your investments. Consulting with a financial advisor can assist you in developing a well-rounded investment strategy that matches your risk tolerance and helps you reach your financial goals.

Habit 7: Failure to Pay Yourself First

Paying yourself first is a financial guideline that is sometimes ignored yet is critical to long-term financial success and security. It entails prioritizing savings and investments for your future over other expenses. Unfortunately, many people develop the practice of not paying themselves first, which can impede wealth growth, postpone financial goals, and cause financial stress. Let's look at why paying yourself first is important, the benefits it provides, and how to put this philosophy into practice for a stronger financial future.

Understanding the Concept of Self-Pay
"Paying yourself first" is a fundamental financial principle that can alter your money management strategy and lead you to

financial security and prosperity. This principle, at its core, highlights the importance of prioritizing savings and investments by devoting a percentage of your income to yourself before addressing other obligations. You can take control of your financial destiny, achieve your goals, and develop a foundation of financial resiliency by adopting this mindset and practice.

The Fundamental Principle

Paying yourself first switches your focus from spending money on immediate wants and desires to putting money aside for long-term goals and financial security. Instead of being an afterthought, saving becomes a purposeful and necessary component of your financial routine. This idea recognizes that you are your most valuable asset, therefore investing in yourself should be a primary priority.

Key Components of Paying Yourself First

- Savings Automation: Automating your savings is a practical approach to applying the philosophy of paying yourself first. Set up direct deposits from your paycheck to selected savings or investment accounts. This ensures that a percentage of your income is saved before it is available for discretionary spending.

- Clear financial objectives: Define precise financial goals that match your dreams, such as saving for an emergency fund, a down payment on a house, or funding your retirement. Having specific goals gives your savings meaning and inspires you to commit to paying yourself first.

- Prioritization and budgeting: Make a budget that takes into account your income, fixed expenses, discretionary spending, and savings goals. As a non-negotiable item in your budget, allocate a predetermined percentage of your income to your savings or investment accounts.

- careful Spending: Adopting a pay-yourself-first mentality promotes careful spending. When you emphasize saving and investing, you become more aware of where your money is going and prevent impulsive or unnecessary expenditures.

- Consistency and Incremental Growth: Begin with a modest amount of your salary and progressively increase it as your financial condition improves. Building the habit and getting the advantages of this exercise requires consistency.

The Advantages of Paying Yourself First

- Financial security: By putting money aside for an emergency fund, you'll be better prepared to deal with unforeseen expenses without going into debt. This gives you financial security and comfort of mind.

- Regular contributions to savings and investments increase over time, allowing you to capitalize on the power of compound interest. This results in tremendous growth and wealth creation, allowing you to meet your long-term financial objectives.

- Goal Achievement: Paying yourself first keeps your financial goals at the forefront of your decisions. You're actively working toward your goals, whether they're to purchase a home, establish a business, or retire comfortably.

- Disciplined Spending: This technique promotes responsible spending habits. You learn to distinguish between necessities and wants, making deliberate decisions that match your financial priorities.
- Reduced Stress: A typical source of worry is financial stress. Paying yourself first creates a financial safety net that allows you to focus on other elements of your life without worrying about money.
- Empowerment: Taking responsibility for your finances by paying yourself first provides you the power to shape your financial future. You take charge of your financial destiny by making well-informed decisions that align with your goals and values.

Paying Yourself First at Various Stages of Life

- Early in your career, prioritize saving for an emergency fund and establishing a sound financial foundation. This serves as a safety net as you deal with job changes and unexpected expenses.
- Mid-Career: As your income grows, allocate a larger percentage of it to retirement accounts and investment portfolios. This is an essential time to increase money creation in order to achieve financial independence in the future.
- Contributions to retirement accounts and investment vehicles that correspond to your retirement timetable should be prioritized. You're preparing for a nice retirement while lowering your need for social security.

- Paying yourself first is still important in retirement. Consistent withdrawals from your retirement assets, combined with cautious budgeting, ensure that you may relax and enjoy your golden years.

Paying yourself first is a basic financial attitude that lays the foundation for financial success and freedom. It requires a mental shift and disciplined activity, but the rewards are great. Prioritizing savings and investments allows you to invest in yourself, build a more secure financial future, and set the way for a life filled with opportunities, stability, and prosperity.

Habit 8: Over-Reliance on Credit

In our consumer-driven culture, credit has become a vital tool for managing money and meeting pressing demands. While credit provides convenience and flexibility, excessive use can result in a number of financial blunders and long-term consequences. From rising debt to decreased financial stability, it's vital to understand the risks of excessive credit use and learn how to strike a healthy balance.

The Pitfalls of Excessive Credit Use

In a world where credit is widely available and consumerism is ubiquitous, the allure of excessive credit usage can lead individuals down a perilous financial path. While credit gives rapid purchasing power and convenience, overusing it can lead to a number of risks that undermine financial stability and impair long-term development. It's vital to realize the risks of excessive credit usage and take proactive steps to avoid them, from increased debt to less financial flexibility.

1. Rising Debt and Interest Rates

One of the most evident repercussions of excessive credit usage is the accumulation of enormous amounts of debt. Using credit cards or loans to cover routine expenses, luxury products, or non-essential purchases can easily spiral into a difficult-to-break borrowing cycle. Interest charges rise in lockstep with credit card balances. Because of the high-interest rates on outstanding accounts, a considerable amount of your monthly payments are used to pay down interest rather than reducing the underlying debt.

2. Financial Concerns and Stress

Excessive credit use can create financial stress and anxiety. Juggling several credit card bills, loan payments, and debt accumulation can lead to a condition of constant anxiety about how to make ends meet. Financial stress can negatively impact one's mental health, relationships, and overall quality of life.

3. Lower Savings and Investing

Using credit frequently leaves little room for saving and investing. Funds that may otherwise be utilized to build an emergency reserve, contribute to retirement accounts, or seek investment opportunities are instead diverted to debt payments. This lack of saving and investing may hinder long-term financial goals and prevent you from achieving financial freedom.

4. A lower credit score

Excessive credit utilization may have a negative impact on your credit score. Carrying significant credit card balances in contrast to your credit limits, skipping payments, or opening many lines of credit in a short period of time can all lead to a worse credit score. A low credit score limits your ability to secure suitable loan terms as well as your access to better financial opportunities.

5. Lack Of Financial Flexibility

Credit reliance may reduce your financial flexibility and impair your ability to adapt to change and capitalize on opportunities. A significant portion of your earnings may be allocated to debt payments, leaving little room for unforeseen obligations, job changes, or new investments.

6. Impaired Long-Term Goals

Excessive credit use may make meeting long-term financial goals challenging. Whether you're buying a house, attending college, or planning for retirement, using credit for short-term goals can hinder your capacity to prepare for these critical milestones.

7. Cycle of Borrowing

Excessive credit use frequently leads to a borrowing cycle. When one credit line runs dry, customers may turn to another to cover current debt, perpetuating a cycle of borrowing and increasing debt burdens.

8. The Impact on Relationships

Excessive credit utilization can put a financial strain on relationships. Money management disagreements, rising debt, and opposing financial agendas can all lead to conflict in homes and marriages.

9. Limited Access to Opportunities

A strong financial foundation enables you to capitalize on opportunities as they emerge. Excessive credit utilization limits your ability to invest in personal growth, education, company, and other efforts that could enhance your financial situation.

10. Lower Overall Happiness

Excessive credit use can have far-reaching consequences that harm one's overall well-being. Financial insecurity and debt can contribute to feelings of overwhelm, hopelessness, and decreased life satisfaction.

Taking a Balanced Approach to Credit Use

To minimize the risks of excessive credit usage, make a concerted effort to strike a balance between permissible credit usage and responsible financial management:

- Budgeting: Create a precise budget that details your income, expenses, and savings objectives. Set aside a modest amount for discretionary expenditures to avoid overspending on credit.
- Build an emergency fund to handle unforeseen needs without having to use credit. During difficult times, an emergency fund serves as a safety net.
- Credit should be treated as a tool rather than a lifeline. Use it for planned purchases or emergencies, and make sure you have a repayment plan in place.
- Debt Repayment: Pay off high-interest bills and credit card balances first. To eliminate debt faster, make more than the minimum payment.

- Financial Education: Learn about personal money, credit management, and debt management solutions. Learning about responsible credit usage gives you the ability to make sound financial decisions.

- Mindful Spending: Practicing mindful spending is examining each purchase and determining whether it is in line with your financial goals and priorities.

- Limit Credit Cards: Avoid amassing many credit cards, and instead select cards with favorable terms and rewards schemes that correspond to your demands.

- Financial Objectives: Establish specific financial objectives and develop a plan for reaching them. Focusing on long-term goals can help to curb impulse buying.

- Professional Assistance: If your debt becomes unmanageable, get professional help from credit counselors or financial experts to build a repayment plan.
- Open Communication: Discuss money issues with family members and partners freely. A common understanding and collaborative efforts can help to limit the consequences of excessive credit consumption.

While credit can be a beneficial financial instrument, overusing it can lead to a slew of issues that affect your financial well-being and your entire quality of life. Recognizing possible traps and taking proactive efforts to appropriately manage credit will help you negotiate the intricacies of today's financial market. You may attain financial security, follow your goals, and construct a future distinguished by resilience, opportunity, and long-term prosperity by taking a balanced approach to credit usage.

Responsible Credit Management and Debt Reduction

When used wisely, credit may be a powerful instrument, allowing people to access funds for crucial purchases, emergencies, and opportunities. However, the key to efficiently leveraging credit is responsible management and meticulous debt reduction techniques. Understanding how to utilize credit sensibly and applying debt-reduction strategies can help you achieve financial freedom and stability.

1. Recognize Your Credit: Begin by learning everything you can about your credit report and credit score. Monitor your credit report regularly to ensure accuracy and to spot any potential problems. Maintaining a healthy credit score is critical since it affects your ability to get favorable loan arrangements.

2. Make a Budget: Create a precise budget that details your monthly earnings, fixed expenses, discretionary spending, and debt commitments. A budget clarifies your financial inflows and outflows, making it easier to allocate funds for debt repayment and other financial objectives.

3. Prioritize High-Interest Debt: Begin by addressing high-interest debt, such as credit card accounts, first. Debt can quickly accrue due to high-interest rates, therefore paying off these bills early will save you a considerable amount of money in interest charges.

4. The Snowball Technique: The snowball technique entails paying off the smallest bills first and making minimum payments on larger ones. When you have paid off the smallest obligation, apply the amount you were paying toward it to the next smallest loan. As you reach each debt milestone, this strategy gives you a psychological boost.

5. Avalanche Technique: The avalanche technique emphasizes debt repayment by paying off the highest-interest loans first. By paying off high-interest bills as soon as possible, you reduce the amount of interest you pay over time and speed up your trip to debt freedom.

6. Debt Consolidation: Combining several high-interest debts into a single, lower-interest loan can simplify repayment while potentially lowering interest rates. When considering debt consolidation, be cautious and make sure the terms are advantageous.

7. Negotiate Interest Rates: Contact creditors to negotiate reduced interest rates, especially if you have a track record of timely payments. Lower interest rates can drastically reduce the total amount owed.

8. Raise Your Income: Look into ways to raise your income, whether through a side hustle, freelance employment, or a part-time job. The extra money can be used to pay off debts.

9. Reduce Unnecessary Expenses: Examine your discretionary spending to see where you may cut back. Redirect the savings toward debt reduction to speed up the process.

10. Pay More Than the Minimum: Pay more than the minimum monthly payment on your debts wherever possible. Even a marginally higher payment can significantly reduce the principal balance.

11. Emergency Reserve: Continue to create or maintain an emergency reserve while focused on debt reduction. An emergency fund keeps you from having to use credit in the event of an unforeseen need.

12. Monitor Progress: To stay motivated, keep track of your progress regularly. Celebrate accomplishments and acknowledge the good impact of your debt-reduction efforts.

13. Seek Professional Assistance: If your debt becomes unmanageable, seek help from credit counseling organizations or financial advisors. They can assist you in developing a structured repayment plan and providing advice on how to manage your financial condition.

14. Avoid New Debt: While working to reduce existing debt, avoid incurring new debt whenever possible. A commitment to proper credit management is abstaining from taking on new responsibilities that could stymie your progress.

15. Develop Financial Discipline: Responsible credit management and effective debt reduction, in the end, necessitate a commitment to financial discipline. It is critical to develop healthy financial habits and exercise self-control when it comes to spending and borrowing.

Credit management and debt reduction are essential components of establishing financial stability and assuring a bright future. You may recover control of your financial situation and move toward debt-free status by understanding how credit works, making a budget, and executing debt-reduction measures. The road to debt independence involves perseverance, drive, and regular effort. Remember that you have power over your financial situation and that with careful credit management and proactive debt reduction measures, you can pave the road for a healthier financial future.

Habit 9: Failing To Save

In the short term, failing to save money may appear insignificant, but the long-term implications can have a big influence on your financial well-being and general quality of life. Saving is more than just setting aside a portion of your money; it's a critical step toward attaining your goals and weathering unanticipated obstacles. Let's look at the consequences of not prioritizing savings and ways for overcoming this typical financial mistake.

Building an Emergency Fund

An emergency fund is a powerful instrument that provides protection and peace of mind during unforeseen life occurrences. Life is full of unplanned expenses, and having a dedicated fund to address them can mean the difference between financial stability and insurmountable debt. Let's look at the significance of having an emergency fund and how to put one together.

The Importance of an Emergency Fund

- Unexpected Expenses: Emergencies, such as medical costs, car repairs, or unexpected job loss, can occur at any time. An emergency fund ensures that you are prepared to deal with financial difficulties without resorting to credit cards or loans.
- Financial stability: An emergency reserve provides financial protection. Knowing you have money set up for unexpected expenses gives you peace of mind and minimizes stress.
- Debt Avoidance: You may be forced to borrow money to cover unexpected bills if you do not have an emergency reserve. This might result in debt

accumulation that is difficult to manage and costly in the long run.

- Maintaining Objectives: An emergency fund protects your financial ambitions from being derailed by unanticipated setbacks. You can stick to your goals, whether they be to buy a home, pay for education, or invest.

Creating an Emergency Fund

- Make a plan: Determine how much money you want in your emergency fund. A good rule of thumb is to save three to six months' worth of living costs.

- Begin Small: If your current financial circumstances make large-scale savings difficult, start with a modest objective and gradually work your way up.

- Set it as a priority: Consider your emergency fund to be a key financial goal. Set aside a portion of your earnings for this fund.

- Set up recurring transfers from your bank account to an emergency fund. This guarantees constant contributions with minimal effort.
- Reduce your discretionary spending: Examine your budget and identify places where you may reduce non-essential spending. Redirect your savings to your emergency fund.
- Make Good Use of Windfalls: Bonuses, tax returns, and unexpected gifts can all contribute significantly to your emergency fund.
- Consistency is essential: Aim for consistent contributions, no matter how modest. These payments compound up over time to a sizable emergency fund.
- Avoid Temptation: Once your emergency fund begins to develop,

resist the need to dip into it for non-urgent expenses.

- Prioritize High-Interest Debt: If you have high-interest debt, consider paying it off before establishing your emergency fund completely. This keeps debt from piling up too soon.

Making Use of Your Emergency Fund

- Actual Emergencies: Only use the fund for true emergencies - unexpected, urgent, and necessary events.
- Medical bills, unexpected healthcare costs, or emergency medical treatments are all appropriate reasons to use your emergency fund.
- Car Repairs: Unexpected car repairs or replacements might be costly, yet they are essential to sustain your daily life.
- Job Loss: If you lose your job or have a decrease in income, your emergency

money can cover your living needs while you look for new options.

- Major household repairs, such as a leaking roof or plumbing problems, are considered emergency expenses.
- Avoid Non-Emergency Expenses: Use the fund just for planned expenses and not for discretionary spending.

Rebuilding Your Emergency Fund:

- Prioritize Replenishment: Make it a priority to replenish your emergency fund as quickly as possible after depleting it.
- Make Budget Changes: Examine your budget to see where you may put money to help restore your emergency fund. Consider shifting discretionary expenditure to savings.
- Maintain Your Commitment: The emergency fund is a perpetual financial

tool. Continue to contribute to ensuring that you are prepared for future unforeseen circumstances.

Finally, establishing an emergency fund is a critical step in achieving financial resilience and stability. Setting money aside for unforeseen needs creates a safety net that protects your financial well-being. Approach the process with patience and devotion, and keep in mind that each donation takes you closer to your ultimate objective of having a trusted resource to help you negotiate life's uncertainties. An emergency fund enables you to meet issues head-on, maintain your financial stability, and look forward to a future of greater confidence and peace of mind.

Long-Term Savings Goals and Strategies

Setting long-term savings goals is a critical component of obtaining financial security and realizing your dreams. Whether you're saving for retirement, purchasing a home, paying for college, or taking a dream vacation, having a clear strategy in place is critical for making your dreams a reality. Let's look at the significance of long-term savings objectives and successful ways of navigating this transforming path.

The Importance of Long-Term Savings Goals

- Creating Financial Clarity: Long-term savings objectives provide a clear path for your financial journey. They assist you in developing a strategy and allocating resources effectively to reach your goals.

- Achieving Goals: Long-term savings objectives enable you to accomplish your aspirations, whether they be to retire comfortably, explore the world, or provide a good education for your children.
- Creating Wealth: Consistent long-term saving permits your investments to expand over time, compounding returns and creating money to support your future efforts.
- Discipline Promotion: Having clear savings goals helps financial discipline. It encourages you to budget, avoid impulsive spending, and prioritize your goals.

Effective Strategies for Meeting Long-Term Savings Objectives:
- Outline Your Goals: Clearly outline your long-term savings objectives.

Having defined goals, whether it's retiring at a certain age, purchasing a home, or supporting your child's school, gives you a feeling of purpose.

- Set Attainable Goals: Set attainable savings goals that are in line with your current financial condition and future salary estimates. Unrealistic goals can cause frustration and discourage continuous saving efforts.

- Divide your long-term ambitions into smaller, doable benchmarks. This makes the journey more manageable and helps you to track progress more efficiently.

- Create a Timeline: Create a timeline for each milestone and the overall goal. Knowing when you want to reach your goals allows you to spend resources effectively and stay on track.

- Make a Savings Plan: Make a thorough savings plan outlining how much you need to save each month to meet your goals. Consider inflation and prospective investment returns.

- Set up automatic transfers from your checking account to selected savings or investment accounts. Automation ensures regular contributions without requiring constant manual effort.

- Choose the Right Accounts: Depending on your goals, consider using several types of accounts, such as retirement accounts (e.g., 401(k) or IRA), investment accounts, or dedicated savings accounts.

- Diversify your investments: If your goals include investing, diversify your portfolio to control risk and maximize possible returns. Consult with a financial expert to ensure that your investing strategy is in line with your objectives.

- Maintain Consistency: Maintaining consistency is essential for reaching long-term savings goals. Maintain your savings plan even during times of financial uncertainty or unanticipated expenses.
- Track Your Progress: Examine your progress toward your savings goals regularly. Use this time to reflect on your accomplishments, make changes, and stay inspired.
- Reevaluate and Adjust: As your life circumstances change, so will your long-term goals. Reevaluate your goals regularly and make changes as appropriate.
- Avoid Lifestyle Inflation: As your income grows, resist the impulse to drastically increase your expenditure.

Set aside a considerable amount of the extra money for long-term savings.

- Reduce your debt: Prioritize debt repayment over long-term savings. High-interest debt might stymie your overall financial success.
- Educate Yourself: Continue to educate yourself on personal finance, investing, and long-term goals. You can make better selections the more informed you are.

Incorporating Long-Term Savings Goals in Your Lifestyle:

Achieving long-term savings objectives takes a combination of strategic planning, commitment, and tenacity. Make these objectives a part of your daily life by incorporating them into your financial routine:

- Milestones should be recognized and celebrated. Each accomplishment puts you closer to your ultimate goal.
- Visual Reminders: Use visual signals, such as vision boards or financial planners, to keep your long-term goals apparent and motivating.
- Reviews regularly: Maintain a regular evaluation of your savings plan to verify you're on track. Adjust your strategies as your living circumstances and financial status change.
- Share Objectives: Discuss your long-term savings goals with family members or a trusted friend. Sharing your goals gives accountability and emotional support.
- Maintain your adaptability: Life may present you with unexpected challenges or possibilities. Maintain flexibility and change your techniques as needed

while keeping your long-term goals in mind.

In conclusion, setting and accomplishing long-term financial goals is a transformative journey that involves devotion, strategy, and regular effort. You may walk the route to financial success by setting your goals, developing successful tactics, and incorporating savings into your daily routine. Long-term savings goals enable you to realize your dreams, accumulate wealth, and experience a future distinguished by security, opportunity, and the fulfillment of your ambitions. Remember that every step you take puts you closer to a brighter and more affluent tomorrow.

Habit 10: Avoiding Financial Planning

Financial planning is frequently disregarded or put off, which can result in many potential errors that could have a severe influence on your financial stability and future. Avoiding financial planning could seem good in the short term, but it can lead to missed opportunities, more stress, and a lack of focus on attaining your financial goals in the long run. Let's examine the dangers of skipping financial planning and the possible repercussions it may have.

The Role of Financial Planning in Achieving Goals

Avoiding financial planning can have negative effects on your financial situation and make it more difficult for you to accomplish your goals in life. Financial planning is a systematic process that gives you the capacity to use resources wisely, make informed financial decisions, and strive toward a stable financial future. It involves more than just setting up a budget. This chapter will examine the crucial role that financial planning plays in helping you achieve your goals and explain why you should adopt this strategy.

1. Matching Your Finances To Your Goals: Your current financial condition and your future ambitions are connected through financial planning. It entails establishing specific objectives, whether they are for purchasing a home, launching a business, paying for your children's school, or retiring comfortably. You acquire clarity on the steps required to transform your ambitions become reality by building a roadmap that describes how you will achieve your goals.

2. Laying a Firm Foundation: Building a strong foundation for a house is similar to financial planning. It guarantees that your financial system is solid and resilient to unforeseen difficulties. You strengthen your financial resilience by evaluating your present financial situation, recognizing prospective risks, and coming up with mitigation plans.

3. Making the Most of Resources: You can more effectively allocate your resources if you have financial planning. It guarantees that every dollar is working toward your goals and has a purpose. Without a plan, you may find yourself making impulsive purchases or skipping out on investment possibilities that may have helped you build your money.

4. Dealing with Risk Management and Debt: A thorough financial plan contains methods for controlling debt and reducing risks. Financial planning makes sure you're ready for the unexpected and can overcome obstacles without stopping your progress, whether it's paying off high-interest debt, creating an emergency fund, or getting the correct insurance coverage.

5. Creating a Plan for Your Life Stage: Your present stage of life is taken into account while budgeting your finances, and techniques are modified accordingly. A well-designed financial plan adapts to your changing circumstances and aids you in making decisions that are in line with your priorities, whether you are starting your career, establishing a family, or nearing retirement.

6. Planning a Retirement Path: Preparing for retirement is one of the most important components of financial planning. A financial plan establishes a strategy to assist you reach that goal by carefully analyzing how much you should save for retirement. Early retirement planning will allow you to take advantage of compound interest and guarantee a comfortable retirement.

How to Create a Customized Financial Plan

- **Define Your Goals First:** Establishing your short- and long-term financial goals should be your first step. Think about your near-term objectives, like purchasing a home or paying off college loans, as well as your longer-term objectives, such as retiring early or launching a business.
- **Evaluate Your Current Circumstance:** Examine your existing financial condition carefully. Subtract your liabilities (debts) from your assets (savings, investments, and real estate) to get your net worth. This gives you a

quick glimpse of your financial situation.

- **Create A Budget:** Make a thorough budget that details your monthly revenue and outgoing costs. Include all costs, including variable costs (groceries, entertainment), fixed costs (rent, utilities), and discretionary spending. A budget shows you where you may make cuts to increase your savings and helps you understand your spending patterns.

- **Establish An Emergency Fund:** Create an emergency fund as part of your financial strategy to pay for unforeseen expenses. Try to budget for three to six months' worth of expenses. When unforeseen situations happen, an emergency fund acts as a safety net and keeps you from incurring debt.

- **Deal With Debt:** Give paying off high-interest debt, such as credit card accounts, a top priority. Spend more money on paying off these loans to have them paid off faster and pay less interest overall.

- **Investment Plan:** Create an investing plan that is in line with your risk appetite and financial objectives. To reduce risk and possibly increase returns on your assets, think about diversifying your holdings. You should look at retirement plans like 401(k)s and IRAs.

- **Plan For Retirement:** Calculate how much you'll need to retire comfortably by determining your ideal standard of living. Include things like prospective medical costs, inflation, and other factors. Regularly fund retirement accounts and benefit from employer-sponsored retirement programs.

- **Insurance Coverage:** Examine your insurance requirements, including those for health, life, and disability insurance. If an unexpected disaster occurs, having the appropriate coverage guarantees that you and your loved ones will be protected.

- **Regular Evaluations And Modifications:** Financial planning is an ongoing process, not a one-off undertaking. Review your financial plan frequently to gauge your progress and make necessary adjustments to your methods. Your financial plan should vary as your life circumstances do.

- **Consult A Professional For Advice:** To assist you in developing a thorough financial strategy, think about speaking with a financial counselor or planner. A specialist can offer individualized advice, assist you in navigating difficult financial issues, and maximize your methods for reaching your objectives.

Avoiding financial planning can affect your financial security and ability to reach your goals in the long run. A personalized financial plan is a compass that directs you toward success, whether your goal is to save for retirement, pay for education, or accomplish any other financial goal. Always keep in mind that every action you take to organize your finances will get you one step closer to accomplishing your goals and ensuring your financial security.

Conclusion

As we come to the end of our exploration of financial habits and their impact on our lives, it's evident that our financial decisions have far-reaching implications. The book "10 Money Habits That Will Keep You Poor Forever" has shed light on the hazards that might stymie your financial progress and provided guidance on constructing a more affluent future. Throughout the book, we've discussed the ten harmful money behaviors that can lead to financial difficulties and obstruct your path to prosperity

When left unchecked, each of these practices can contribute to a cycle of financial misery. However, armed with the correct knowledge and tactics, you can break free from these patterns and chart a road toward a healthier financial future.

Your commitment to building excellent money habits is the key to long-term wealth. You lay the groundwork for success by embracing financial education, diversifying your income sources, living within your means, tracking your expenses, adopting a wealth-oriented mindset, investing wisely, paying yourself first, managing credit responsibly, saving consistently, and developing a comprehensive financial plan.

Remember that change takes time and effort.t. Small, persistent steps can lead to big changes in your financial life. Focus on one habit at a time, gradually incorporating beneficial habits into your everyday routine. Seek help, educate yourself, and don't be hesitant to seek professional help if necessary.

Keep your goals in mind as you embark on your journey to financial well-being. Visualize the life you want to live and the financial independence you desire. Building wealth, protecting your retirement, caring for your family, or simply enjoying peace of mind will all benefit from your commitment to excellent money habits.

Finally, keep in mind that you can shape your financial future. You may break free from the behaviors that keep you locked in financial difficulty with information, commitment, and a willingness to make positive changes. Accept the principles from this book and allow them to lead you to a life of success, security, and fulfillment. Your financial journey is a marathon, not a sprint, and by taking the proper measures now, you're laying the groundwork for a more lucrative and fulfilling tomorrow.

www.ingramcontent.com/pod-product-compliance
Lightning Source LLC
Chambersburg PA
CBHW070846260726
48661CB00004B/1262